LOOKING FOR
SUNSHINE

> A Practical Guide for Dealing
> with Life's Challenges

Jeff Pasquale

The information contained in this book is intended to be educational and not for diagnosis, prescription, or treatment of any health disorder whatsoever. This information should not replace consultation with a competent healthcare professional. The content of this book is intended to be used as an adjunct to a rational and responsible health care program prescribed by a healthcare practitioner. The author and publisher are in no way liable for any misuse of the material.

More information about Jeff can be found at www.JeffPasquale.com.

Editor: Kammy Wood

Text layout and design: Fagaras Codrut Sebastian

Cover design: Vanessa Nicole Ortiz

Contents

Introduction

~

Sunshine, it seems, is most elusive in our lives when we need it the most. Of course I'm not talking about real sunshine in this case, but spiritual sunshine – its light, brightness, and illumination – that helps reveal the essentials of life that seem to fade away when we're in trouble.

Current events, both global and local, are becoming more and more overwhelming as we collectively try to comprehend what is happening to us, around us, and to each other. When you couple these external events with our own personal challenges, it's not surprising to see that drug companies are enjoying all-time high profits for their lines of sleep-inducing, anxiety-removing, and pain-reducing elixirs.

If you're reading this book, then you are likely searching for a path to peace, tranquility, or problem-resolution. Realistically, though, a book can't fully solve your problems, but it can offer you options as you start on your quest. This book's purpose is to set you on a path to find ways to deal with your challenges, and help with the feelings of hopelessness that are usually associated with these challenges.

This book is intended for anyone who feels alone or lost in a sea of problems.

When that sense of loneliness strikes you, read a chapter.

When that feeling of helplessness overcomes you, read a chapter.

I don't mean to sound facetious or cocky. I write these words for myself as much as for others, because I have had those same feelings, and I too forget where to seek help.

When times are tough, we tend to seek out a safe place, a destination that we can move towards that will enable us to see things more clearly — and, hopefully, begin to put things into perspective.

A good many people believe that they must solve their problems on their own. That belief often originates as a family tradition learned from an early age. That tradition holds that outsiders are not allowed to see the family's problems, or dirty laundry. Often, it's not the fear of exposure that cripples us with inaction, but our own sense of defeat, shame, and pride, which prevents us from opening up and seeking help. Instead we try to do it ourselves, with the hope that things will get better.

This is not a religious book but a spiritual one. Its origins come from the belief that we are never alone. And in times of stress and uncertainty, it seems to be much harder to believe this is true.

The challenge we all face is our inclination to immediately try to solve our problems through physical, mental, and nervous energy. These methods work for us as long as our problems occur randomly, and not simultaneously or sequentially; our inner strength enables us to persevere without incident.

But what about those times when problems do come simultaneously, and with severity?

What then? That's what this book is about; not the random, infrequent problems that we all experience from time to time in our lives, but those crippling, multiple challenges that come crashing down upon us like big waves while you're stuck ankle deep in sand and can't get away.

When you are not clear about who you are and what you believe in, you may feel that your world is spinning out of control when a big problem strikes. When you become separated from God, it's easier to feel alone and punished when a big problem occurs. What you need is a portal to that part of you that became disconnected from God – your light, your center, your spirit. The good news is, despite how you feel or what you think, you are not disconnected from God; you've just been looking in the wrong places.

Pain, whether it's physical or emotional, is the great equalizer among us all because we all must go through it. So if you still feel that you've been singled out with your problems, it's time to let that belief go.

It may seem unfair that sunshine is sometimes elusive and that pain is unavoidable but the reality is even on a cloudy day the sun is shining; we need to actively look for and recognize that light, no matter where we are and what we are going through, is always in us, around us, and above us.

Sunshine (or light) is inside each one of us. It helps us understand and accept who we are and what we are. This light within us is God's light.

Your light has the ability to guide you. It will help you attain balance in your life, it will improve your connection to God, and it will improve your ability to see beyond your problems.

To be guided by your light is to be guided by God.

It's important to note that there are steps you can take right now that will reduce the likelihood of your problems getting bigger. These steps are proactive by design and will help enhance your life and improve the lives of those around you:

- Don't tolerate the big stuff or the little stuff. If it's bothering you, deal with it.
- Be complete with everything you do. Don't leave any loose ends.
- Improve your integrity. Be clear and upfront in everything you do.

- Refocus your life on what you most value.
- Strengthen the ties with your family, friends, and community.

These are simple, everyday steps you can take anytime you choose — especially when you see clouds forming on the horizon.

It's important to remember, you're not alone.

> *"If you knew Who walks beside you on the way that you have chosen, fear would be impossible."*
> (pg. 378 — A Course in Miracles)

Centering Prayer #1

～

God, though I sometimes feel ill-prepared and incapable of helping myself, I hereby commit to You and to myself that I will try.

I know that we are all different. From person to person, we each are blessed with our own unique qualities, capabilities, capacities, and purposes. Although I am different from her, and he is different from me, we still share many of the same capacities – to love, to think, to feel, to intend, and to try. Where we differ is in the degree of willingness we intend to work at our fullest capacity to resolve our problems.

God, help me to find the willingness I know I was born with to be fully aware and responsible for my actions in resolving my challenges, even if I do not believe I am up to the task.

My spirit is Your spirit. Help me to find my true spirit, that light within me that comes from You.

I don't ask for thoughts of comfort or reassurance; I ask only that You help me to help myself, in my time of need.

1.   Move Towards What INSPIRES You

~

This chapter requires action on your part.

The action is that you seek to be inspired.

In times of distress, it's easy to become disoriented, discouraged, or distant — so what you need is the ability to connect to an immediate source of positive energy. Not the energy that gives comfort and reassurance, but the kind of energy that lifts you up to a higher place.

If you're like most people, you are probably seeking a quick solution to your problem. Quick solutions rarely work, and worse, they can replace one problem with another. A quick fix usually results in stepping right over (or on top of) those things that will inspire you to find the right solution.

Think about this for a moment – when you're troubled or worried, usually the last thing you look for is something that will make you happy. Inspiration can make you happy.

Inspiration takes you out of your head and into your heart and soul, to a place where higher ideals and standards live and breathe. When you are in this place, you see things more clearly and with less emotion, which is really where you want to be when problems seem insurmountable.

Inspiration is unique because you can't measure it and you can't see it, but you certainly know when it's not there.

Like a moth to a flame, it tends to be our nature to place intense focus on the fact that we have a problem. It's more of an automated response than a conscious decision on our part, so rather than looking for a source of joy, we choose to swim in our sea of pain, crying out to others, or silently to ourselves, "Look at the problems I've got!"

Some of us seek to be distracted when a problem shows up, somehow believing that by ignoring it, the problem will be limited or lessened. We fool ourselves into believing that everything will be okay because, in truth, we do not want to deal with it. The truth is that a real shift or breakthrough can only occur when we are inspired to take consistent action — or if we get extremely lucky and the problem resolves itself. Don't count on the latter, take action.

When challenges arise, move instinctively towards those things that inspire you. We all have been inspired by someone or something at one time in our lives. That inspiration made us want to do something better or to be a better person; it moved us. Inspiration gives us a sense of connectedness to God; connectedness to positive feelings…feelings of being a part of something that is good in the world. In plain words, inspiration can lift us out of the funk that we're in.

Sometimes it's a person that inspires us, by either their actions or their words. We are moved to a higher place or a more noble position, making

us aware that greatness comes in all shapes and sizes.

Inspiration is not exclusively a religious term, but it is always a spiritual one. To be inspired is to be "in spirit." When you are inspired, you are living and operating at a higher level of responsiveness to your situation and environment.

> *"Before you can inspire with emotion, you must be swamped with it yourself.*
> *Before you can move their tears, your own must flow.*
> *To convince them, you must yourself believe."*
> — Winston Churchill

Inspiration comes from many sources – other people, books, music, nature, even a story you recently heard.

Sometimes the best way to illustrate a point is to show the opposite. Contrast gives perspective. With inspiration, it's no different.

For example, think of someone who is not inspiring at all to you; in fact, you find them distasteful or repulsive. Do you think you could ever be inspired by that person in the future?

The great thing about inspiration is that you can go looking for it. You can seek it out and allow yourself to be inspired on a regular basis. You especially need this ability when you are overwhelmed or in crisis. At those times, seeking inspiration needs to be almost an automatic response – a conscious decision and a focused effort.

When you raise your awareness level and really intend to find it, inspiration will occur more

frequently. The ideal approach is to seek to be inspired by virtually anyone who crosses your path. It could be the lady who works at the dry cleaners, the man that delivers your mail, or one of your coworkers. They all have the ability to inspire you…if you are looking for it.

And don't look for profound, awe-inducing inspiration. Seek simple, everyday inspiration, the kind that comes from a knowing glance, a gracious word when none is required, or a helping hand when one is needed.

When you feel inspired, you will be able to look at your situation more constructively, more accurately, and with less emotion. Again, inspiration won't solve your problem, but it will lead you to a solution more quickly and effectively.

Ways to actively seek inspiration:

1. Read a book about an inspiring individual or event.
2. Listen to music that inspires you.
3. Watch a movie that inspires you.
4. Become very connected to your environment – especially outdoors. Find a quiet spot and place your focus on nature.
5. Take frequent "time outs" to reflect, meditate, or just be still.

Considerations:

- When was the last time you felt inspired? What caused it? How long did it have an effect on you?
- Can you call to mind a friend, family member, or coworker whom you found to be inspiring? Why? Did you tell them how you felt?
- In what ways or areas could you seek to be inspired more frequently?
- Who is the person that has inspired you the most in your life?

2. Your Situation IS YOURS

~

When I became entrenched in plethora of problems at one point in my life, my coach (and friend) said to me (loudly), "It's your mess, own it!" And that was the beginning and the end of our coaching session.

Okay, you may be asking, so how does one go about owning a problem? While it's true that there's not a training manual on the subject, there are clues all around us as to how to do it.

First, consider our culture. In American culture we love to blame others, shifting responsibility to someone or something else. It happens on a daily basis right before our eyes. People openly blame the government, their spouses, their parents, their jobs, their bosses, their neighbors, and even their churches for the problems they have. These are all examples of avoidance.

Avoidance is a classic human response, and we all do it in one form or another. There's a good side to avoidance and a bad one. In a practical context, it can actually be quite helpful, especially when you're trying to manage your time and you refuse to answer the telephone. We choose to avoid things on a daily basis so we can be more effective in other areas. So we don't immediately respond to every email we receive, every ringing doorbell, or every invite to a party. We're not avoiding out of rudeness; we're trying to keep our balance.

But it's a different story when you're in crisis. Avoidance compounds problems exponentially. Your mind won't let you fully comprehend this fact. It just skips over the eventual consequence in order to get you through the moment to avoid pain.

I once worked with someone whose approach to business problems was very linear. He would diagram his problem on a piece of paper by turning a sheet of paper lengthwise and describing the problem on the far left hand side of the page. On the far right side of the page, he would list potential solutions the problem. He then would choose the most probable and effective solution and go about resolving the problem.

Any ideas he came up with as potential solutions were jotted down in the open space in the center of the page between the problem and the solutions.

Yes, life just isn't that simple for really big problems, but here's a spin on the above process that just might work for you.

Do the exact same thing that my coworker did by listing your problem and potential solutions on a sheet of paper. Now odds are, you won't come up with the perfect solution that is immediately doable. In fact, the solutions you list might not be doable at all because of a lack of resources – a lack of time, ability, contacts, or money, for example.

Now that open space in the middle of your problem/solutions page is where you're going to start listing some actions you can take that will allow you to begin tackling your problem on your

terms and in your timeframe. Call it "the middle ground." In this space, you can begin to address your problem a little more formal, and by raising your awareness about the possibilities.

Now take action; own your situation. You may not have brought the problem upon yourself, but only you can be responsible for removing it. This is not to say you can't get outside help or support, but you must be the person ultimately responsible for initiating and managing the solution.

Said another way – You own the problem AND the solution. Therefore, you cannot and may not delegate your problem, or its solution, to someone else.

Take the first possible action item on your list.

Make that your focus point for the day. Don't let it overwhelm you. If it's a big step like confronting someone you're intimidated by, skip this one and go to the next. Eventually you'll need to address this action item but forcing yourself to take the biggest leap as your first step might be too big of a leap.

Finding ways to remind yourself that you own your problem is a concrete approach to becoming more responsible and aware of what you must do to resolve your "stuff." Use your problem/solutions page as a reference tool to keep you focused on solutions. The more you refer to it, the more solutions begin to appear. Sometimes you'll find answers through process-of-elimination. At other points solutions may appear because you forced yourself to be on the lookout for them.

To move forward and fully own what is happening in your life, stop blaming. Stop blaming yourself, stop blaming other people, and stop blaming circumstances. Blaming yourself is not a way of owning your problem. Blame will not solve your problems and it will not make you feel better.

Look for solutions, try them, test them, move yourself towards resolution. When you own your problem, you should be too busy working on the solution to be searching for someone or something to blame.

The action required in this chapter is two-fold. First, you must wholly own your problem – mentally and spiritually. Second, you must take action on your solutions. Owning your problem is being responsible. And being responsible

will make you feel more capable of solving
your problem.

Ways to understand and own
your situation:

1. Perform a linear outline of your situation.
   Define and breakdown the problem and
   identify the possible solutions to the
   problem. Then take action.
2. Catch yourself blaming; it usually happens
   unconsciously. Raise your awareness level
   and stop yourself as soon as you start.
3. Take responsibility for your situations but
   don't blame yourself. If you caused it, you
   caused it. It's now time to take action to
   undo the situation.
4. Start hanging out with people who don't
   have big problems.

Considerations:

- Take a moment and go back to a time when you didn't have your problem. What did it feel like? What made it feel different?
- It's good to seek counsel from others who have been through similar experiences, but avoid the habit of sharing your situation with people. It's easy to get caught up in the "I-need-other-people's-sympathy" syndrome. Share, but share selectively.

Centering Prayer #2

~

God, I am a good person. I try, I feel, I care. I know that I am blessed to be alive, but I don't always feel that way because I hurt. I want to resolve my problem fully, not just quickly, and I ask for Your help in doing this.

Though I have tried in the past to help myself and deal with my situation, I ask that You help me find the inspiration and the motivation I need to get into action and resolve my problem.

While at times I may feel alone, I know this is only my mind working against me. Grant me the wisdom, the patience, and the clarity I need to resolve my problem.

Help me to remind myself often that You are always near.

Thank you for the blessings that are all around me. I know that the beauty that surrounds me comes from You.

3.   Sense, Out of Nonsense

∾

Though your world may seem upside down at the moment, it wasn't always that way. We all have had periods of clarity, balance, and certainty in our lives, however brief they might be. Though you may feel a million miles away from those elusive feelings of clarity, balance, and certainty right now, deep down, you must know that you will experience them once again.

Sometimes, when you stop trying so hard to find the answer, it shows up by itself. This probably sounds a lot like a movie script, but it's true. When you try to force things to happen on your terms, on your timetable, you may actually end up going backwards. Don't interpret this as advice telling you to stop trying. It's not. The request is to stop trying so hard.

There is a saying that "Control is an illusion," meaning that we rarely have full control over events and situations; there are just too many variables and outside factors. Yes, this is a generalization, but at the heart of it lies a speck of truth. If your world really is upside down, then trying to make sense out of it may be more confusing and difficult, if not painful.

Sometimes, while trying hard to understand the things that have happened in your life, you rationalize and dissect things to the point of ridiculousness. Like some of the old world beliefs that live on to this day, such as believing that if you spill salt or break a mirror, you'll have

bad luck — or if you shower or bath on a full stomach you'll get sick — we come up with an explanation for the craziness in our lives when there is no reason for it. It just is.

Yes, it is important to understand what is happening to you, but rationalizing the causes only complicates finding the correct solution. Consider the simple causes, not to make it easy on yourself, but to give you time to focus on resolving the problem.

Just as you need to accept the situation you're in as yours, you also need to accept the fact that you may never know why something has happened to you. Accept that crazy things can and do happen to normal people, and that's that. Simplistic? Yes. But sometimes the most effective and expedient thing to do is just accept what's happening and move on.

When you move to a deeper level of acceptance, you come to the understanding that you are ultimately in control of your responses to the things that happen to you.

You don't have to sing or dance or celebrate the fact that you have a problem, but you don't have to come unglued or immobilized because of it, either. And that's where making sense of things comes in. You see, the sense is not in understanding the problem, the sense is in understanding yourself and why you respond to things the way you do.

Have you ever been overtaken by a friend or loved one who told a story with such panic and urgency that you became passionate and excited, too? We all can be affected and overcome with this strong sense of urgency about something. It has nothing to do with us and yet there we are,

as excited as if the problem was exclusively ours. And yet, only minutes before, you were calm and happy. The secret to dealing with these kinds of situations is to offer a peaceful response.

You, no doubt, know people who always seem in control and peaceful while they are experiencing an amazing amount of pressure or problems. The reality is, these individuals have learned the skill of staying focused on what's truly important to them. Most likely this is because they've figured out exactly what is important to them in life and why.

One of the strongest examples of this kind of purpose and focus is in professional sports. Consider an important game-winning serve in tennis, or a tie-breaking foul shot in basketball, or a baseball pitcher's all important, game-winning third strike in the World Series. Each of these scenes typically takes place amidst thousands of fans and millions of television viewers, and yet, despite the pandemonium around them, each player is seemingly oblivious to his or her surroundings. These are examples of the power of purpose and focus in action. That's the power of making sense out of what you're doing despite what's going on around you.

Obviously, to perform at the level a professional athlete takes a lot of practice, but for your purposes, all you need to do is choose what to focus on and learn how to stay focused on resolving your problem; you make sense out of the nonsense around you by moving forward.

Whenever I feel incapable of understanding what's going on around me, I think of the words Stephen Covey told me when I met him for the first time. I had asked him a question about how

to positively influence a company that I didn't run. He simply replied – "Work on your circle."

I believe the same approach works when you want to influence yourself, especially when you're surrounded by trouble. So what is this circle that Covey is talking about?

He first described this concept in his book, "The 7 Habits of Highly Effective People." This circle is your circle of influence; within it are those people or circumstances that you have the ability to affect or influence. This circle is typically surrounded by a circle of concern, which contains those things you have absolutely no power or control over. The intention is, the more you focus on and pay attention to those people and things in your circle of influence, the bigger that circle gets and the smaller that circle of concern is.

Gaining or regaining your sense of purpose probably feels like an impossible task right now. As you approach a resolution to your problem, consider finding a way to accept your problem as yours, and a way of working on your circle of influence. Consider the truth about your situation and what you need to do about it. Get clear. Stay focused. Accept your situation. Work on your circle.

Ways to make sense out of things:

1. Identify those people in your life that you consider to be in your Personal Circle of Influence. How do you help them? How do they help you?

2. Identify those people in your life that you consider to be in your Circle of Influence at work. How do you help them? How do they help you?

3. What types of hobbies/activities do you like to do? If you're not sure, make a list. Then start doing them more often. Daily, if necessary.

4. What things – people, places, and events – make you feel more at peace or in balance? See those people, go to those places, or do those things more frequently.

Considerations:

- Make a list of those things in your life that make you feel good. The list might only consist of one or two items right now, but write them down. Review them each day.
- Learn to appreciate again, or more frequently. Consciously knowing what you appreciate forces you to take stock in what you have – no matter how much or how little. We all have people and things in our lives that we appreciate. Make it a morning or evening ritual to consciously appreciate.
- Identify those things in your life that you can control. Relationships (your part in them, that is), quality of your work, amount of rest and exercise, quality of your diet, etc.
- Catch yourself when you've just been completely immersed and focused on

something. Learn to recognize when and how often it happens. When it does, this is you making sense out of your life – even if you were immersed in reading a magazine or walking down the street. Sense comes from purposeful living, and sometimes by doing the simplest things.

4. Recognize and Understand Your Fears

~

If you allow them, your fears will take you to places you'd never wish to go. A lot of people don't really understand why they feel the way they do about things, they just respond automatically. Fear is one of those feelings.

Many times we fail to recognize the knot in our stomach is not dread or stress, it's simply fear. Fear can be crippling, and fear can be overwhelming, but fear can be controlled and even conquered.

The causes of fear are many. It could be shame, or pride, or vanity, for example. Which is why it is important to know what's really important to you. What's driving you. Sometimes you think you've got your priorities straight when in reality they are completely out of balance.

Fear can be derived from a sense of loss – a loss of status, a loss of possessions, a loss of income, even a loss of identity. Either consciously or unconsciously, you have placed such a high value on that "thing" you're so afraid of losing that it triggers physical and emotional stress.

It's interesting to note that fear is a primary ingredient for the majority of today's advertising and marketing. It's sometimes subtle, but advertising messages will tend to lean on *don't-be-left-out* or *don't-be-left–behind* concepts. People in general, hate to miss out on something, and that

means that if they don't buy now, they'll miss out. Their neighbors will have something they don't. Fear is a trigger point for many things.

It is important to understand that while the event, situation, or result that you're worried about may not exist or ever come true, the feelings of fear and dread are very real. Those feelings hurt because they're real. The reality is that everything you perceive in life causes an emotional response. From the smallest gesture from a friend to the most horribly obnoxious thing a family member might say, they all evoke some kind of emotional response.

Fear is an emotion, a driving force. Fears usually originate when we're children. Because most adults try to control their children through fear, we arrive at adulthood with an unhealthy set of fears.

Some of those fears are legitimate cautions –
"Stay away from the electric outlet, you could get
hurt," or "Don't go near the ledge," and so on.
But other fears are less than logical: "Don't go
near the lake, there are monsters in it," or "If you
keep doing that, Daddy will be very mad at you."
Now, it's true that we all eventually grow up and
come to realize that there are no monsters in the
lake, but the more subtle warning – Daddy will
be very mad at you – strikes a raw nerve in every
child. That raw nerve is approval.

It starts with our parents, and next with our
teachers, and if left unchecked, it will continue on
with our boss and our friends. The driving force
of winning another person's approval can create
a lifetime of fear: fear of not being liked and fear
of rejection. These are very real fears when we're
children because our world is dependent on our
parents and then teachers when we're growing up.

If you've ever known someone who was constantly overeager to please, the origins of that tendency can sometimes come from fear.

Regardless of its origins, fear will also show up in our lives as big or little judgments about ourselves or about others and what we consider good or bad.

If you pile up enough of these judgments (big or small, or good or bad), and those judgments are directed against you ("How could I be so stupid?" "I always say the wrong thing," "I waste too much time," "I should be earning more money," etc.), you have created a recipe for feeling horrible. And if one of those bad feelings is fear, there's a really good chance that you're also feeling helpless and unable to take action.

There are many methods for reducing or eliminating fear, but the first important steps are to recognize that fear is there, that you feel it, and that you need to get rid of it. If you fully acknowledge the fear, you are going to fully resolve your problem.

We all have that little voice in our heads that is always reminding us that we're not good enough – not smart enough, not fast enough, not skinny enough, not good-looking enough, or not connected enough. In your current situation, maybe the voice is telling you that you'll never get out of the mess that you're in. This kind of self-talk goes on in everyone's heads.

The solution to stopping the noise of judgment and the seeds of fear is silence. You can begin practicing silence. It's not meditating; but simple

good old-fashioned quiet and solitude. No distractions; just silence.

It begins with the deliberate intent to seize the moment and actively seek opportunities where you can tune things out. In other words, look for solitude, and when you've found it, practice shutting off your mind.

At first you may need to do this on a schedule in order to discipline yourself to seek silence on demand. In time you will find yourself seeking a "time out" for yourself during breaks at work, on the train, or before you go to bed. It will begin to happen without thought.

Practicing silence can be done practically anywhere and at any time but it best occurs in a quiet spot with the sincere intention to stop thinking. You can do this by closing your eyes and counting your breaths, or concentrating on the colors your mind begins to see behind your eyelids, or even imagining puffy white clouds floating by in the sky...no thoughts, no judgments, no fears — just clouds.

Silence allows for other things to happen in your life, namely not to obsess about your fears or your problems. It also creates more open spaces in your head for ideas and opportunities to begin popping up; you're no longer immobilized by fear, you've now quieted your mind for calm to return.

The reality is we all have fears, so it's important to quickly recognize when fear rears its head. See it for what it is and move on. Remember not to let fear define who you are and what you do. You certainly cannot ignore fear, but you can take proactive steps to keep it in check and allow yourself to move beyond it.

Ways to understand your fears:

1. Recognize when you are feeling afraid. Consciously ask yourself why you feel this way or exactly what it is you think you're afraid of.

2. Make a list of activities that help you feel more confident. Confidence might seem like a fleeting sensation but we all have instances where we can consciously make this happen.

3. What is your definition of fear? Why does it have such power over you?

4. There are many sources of fear. What is/ are yours?

Considerations:

- Make a list of your fears, or what you believe are your fears. What are their sources? How do they come to be? Some people fear death, physical harm or impairment, financial distress, loss of a relationship, loss of a job, or just plain embarrassment.
- Find that place where you can go – a room in your house, the park, a church – where you know you can find silence. Silence will overpower fear, but you must let it. Relish the silence. Seek it out, not to hide from people or your problems, but to find a place where you can take care of yourself and not let your problems overpower and overrule you.

5.   Never Doubt Your Value

∼

Are you at a point in your life where everything seems to be going wrong? From your car to the appliances, from your relationships to your finances, nothing seems to be working. If so, you need to understand and acknowledge that this happens even to the brightest and the best-organized individuals. Being told that you're in good company probably doesn't make you feel any better, but the plain truth is that bad stuff happens…to everyone.

And if you are going through a period of personal or professional chaos, one of the last things you'll probably think of is taking a moment to recognize that you are appreciated by others.

I watched a reality show on television recently that granted a terminally ill man, who was still physically active, the opportunity to do a few adventurous activities that were on his "bucket list." Each day for a week, the man was taken somewhere around the country for a different experience. Flying, skiing, and parachuting were some of the activities he participated in.

The show culminated with a surprise gathering of about a hundred family members, friends, neighbors, and associates, all of whom gathered to applaud and acknowledge this man's life and his effect on them. You could see the feeling of shock and humility flash across his face as he voiced the same sentiments to them.

Now you may never have such an opportunity to be acknowledged in unison by the people you have touched, but that doesn't mean that there are not people out there who feel that way about you. As undeserving as you may feel, over the years you must have inspired, shared feelings, or helped more than a few people. My guess is that the actual number of individuals who benefited from this is probably more numerous than you think.

We all tend to discount our own actions, be they good or bad. We don't stop to think that the kind word we offered at the right moment or the helpful action we performed in a time of need could actually affect someone in a positive way. But it can; it does.

> *"The deepest principle in human nature is the craving to be appreciated."* — William James

Similar to inspiration, feeling appreciated tends to increase as we actively appreciate others.

Think back over this past week.

- Who has shown or given you the courtesy of their time or counsel?
- Who went out of their way to help or support you, even when you didn't ask for help?

Start to make a list. It might have been as simple as another person letting you go first in line or someone brought you a cup of coffee; it doesn't matter if the gesture was big or small — list it.

Consciously think about what each person did for you and why you valued or appreciated their action.

There could be one name on your list or twenty. Numbers don't count here. What matters is that you consciously appreciate other people, whether you know them or not.

If you know them, the next step is to contact them. Call them, write them a short note of thanks, or pay them a visit, just as long as you tell them how you felt about their help and why. By doing this, you, in turn, will be valued and appreciated for your effort. This is how it comes back to you.

Conversely, pay attention when someone says "thank you" to you.

- What did you do?
- Was your response a conscious or unconscious one?
- Could you/would you take the time to do this more often for others?

This isn't an exercise in attention-getting. You're not expected to run around town opening doors for people just so you can feel valued and appreciated. Rather, you want to *consciously* be aware of what you do *naturally* because you care.

It's the simple gestures that are more quietly appreciated. It could be making cookies for the kids or soup for the neighbor who is sick. It doesn't matter what you do or for whom, the fact is you are valued for who you are, which means it is the intention behind the action that is appreciated, not the gesture itself.

There are many ways to get value out of your life, but the primary way is to give of yourself. That is, give value (your time, your assistance, your concern, your guidance) to others. By giving value you gain value in your life.

> *You don't find meaning in your life;*
> *you add meaning to your life.*

When you are feeling overwhelmed or less than happy, consciously choose to help someone else. Forget about yourself and your troubles; just do something for someone else.

Ways to know you are valued and appreciated:

1. Pick one day this week to consciously make an effort to do something extra nice for everyone who crosses your path. Be sincere about it; don't fake it. Hold the door, let a fellow driver into your lane, pick up something someone has dropped, etc.

2. Pick another day and consciously recognize and keep track of every time someone is extra nice to you. Appreciate each time it happens and recognize how special it really is.

Considerations:

- In what little ways do you provide value (a kind word or action, a small courtesy, or a helping hand) to:
  - ○ Your family?
  - ○ Your neighbors or your community?
  - ○ Your coworkers?
- In what areas of your life, outside your home, could you be more appreciative of the value or kindness that others give you?

Centering Prayer #3

~

Sometimes, Lord, I am unaware of the good things around me because I am not paying attention. I also fall prey to the common belief that "I should get everything I want, now."

I forget that I can create good in my life by simply doing good.

Help me to better see the value that is all around me in my life, and help me to understand that things will not always occur by my timetable.

Help me, also, to take the time necessary to recognize the value that others bring to my life, as well as the value that I can bring to others. I know how easy it is to not see it, if I'm not looking for it.

6. Your Spirit IS Your Source of Wonder

~

We all can remember a time in our lives when we felt a sense of wonder about someone or something. Unfortunately, most of those experiences occurred when we were children.

Wonder is that unique combination of feelings – one part curiosity, one part appreciation, one part amazement, and another part just being thrilled.

There are other components, to be sure, but wonder usually occurs at those special times in our lives when we are open to discovery and appreciating new things. We are most open to feeling a sense of wonder when we're children. As kids, we are curious, innocent, and non-judgmental; our spirit is clear and unencumbered. But as we get older, we become more heavily influenced by popular opinion, and our spirit's ability to discover, accept, and love is diminished.

I once heard a story (or urban myth) about a three-year-old boy who begs his parents to speak with his newborn baby brother alone. His parents allow him to but they stay close by and eavesdrop, only to hear their three-year-old say to the baby brother, "Tell me about heaven...I think I'm forgetting." Could this be the point at which most of us start to lose our sense of wonder?

Your spirit has much to do with who you are, how happy you are, and how open you are to feeling

wonder-full. Seeking sunshine when you're feeling it's dark all around you is the perfect time to connect with your spirit, the light inside of you that illuminates all that is good in your life. Your spirit (your light) is from God.

Your spirit is visible in others by certain qualities and behaviors that you exude – your energy and enthusiasm, your intention to live by high standards, and the love, caring, and concern that you show for others. When you witness these qualities and behaviors in other people, they can create a sense of wonder in people without effort.

Also, do not confuse spirit with religion. In times of trouble your spirit is your higher power; your connection to God. Your spirit is what guides you most of the time, whether you are conscious of it or not. Your spirit (your light) will always be not only your source of wonder, but the source of your noblest thought, your best intention, your greatest happiness, your deepest sense of empathy, or your most exemplary action.

Think back, if you can, to those people and events that once filled you with wonder. It could have been the boundless optimism of one of your parents. It could have been an amazing athletic or musical performance, or simply the awe you may have felt holding a newborn baby in your hands.

As adults, we still have the capability to sense wonder. Although it happens spontaneously, you can increase your chances of it happening to you if you allow your spirit to shine through. As you would with inspiration, actively seek or think back upon those people and things that filled you with a sense of wonder.

Many people stop dreaming and feeling a sense of wonder after being told for so many years to come back down to earth and face reality. Some people comply with such requests, feeling they should not ignore those whom they respect. But how you reached that place is less important than how you can get back to feeling a sense of wonder.

Realistically, that sense of wonder should begin with you. Whoever you are and whatever you've done (or not done), you are still a miracle. No matter how numb or hurt you currently feel, lift up one of your hands in front of your face and make a fist. Hold it tight and shake it a little. Now slowly, gently release it in front of your face. Repeat the action several times, and consciously be aware of how the thoughts in your brain cause your hand to contract and expand on command.

There are other mammals and animals that have the capability to use their hands on command, to eat, to drink, and to fight, but none can sit alone and think, "How am I able to do this? By what magical force am I able to conceive of an idea in my head, and then through focused action, am able to create and do these things?"

There is cause for wonder in most everything you do or say. To create a sentence, to drive a car, to care for someone else, or to care for yourself — these are all things of wonder.

These simple abilities possessed only by the amazing creations called man and woman are not intended to cause you to sit up and scream — "Wow!" You already should know how unique you are. But feeling that you are unique versus just knowing it is as different as night and day.

Because of this uniqueness, you can also recognize your ability to define and sort out what's troubling you. While this may sound painful, it's the first step you can take that doesn't require you to risk anything or to put yourself at risk, because all you are doing is taking a good look at yourself.

Another dimension of your spirit is your sense of curiosity and discovery. Not the compulsive *I-have-to-have-all-my-questions-answered* type of inquisitiveness but the "I'm genuinely curious" kind. It comes from a recurring feeling of wanting to know more about things you feel are important, and sometimes not so important.

This kind of curiosity unveils wonder because it is a solid part of who you are, and the universe is yours to discover.

So, the question is: what killed or suppressed your sense of wonder? Did you simply allow it to happen slowly over time or was it shut down after an extreme event or experience in your life? Don't think too hard on this one. Pose the question and patiently wait for the answer. Don't force it, it will come.

Allow yourself to periodically reflect on things that you're curious about but have not taken the time to investigate.

> *"The most beautiful thing we can experience is the mysterious. It is the source of all true art and all science. He to whom this emotion is a stranger, who can no longer pause to wonder and stand rapt in awe, is as good as dead: his eyes are closed."*
> — Albert Einstein

Ways to see that your spirit is your source of wonder:

1. Think back to last time you felt a strong sense of wonder. Was it when you were a child, or have you experienced wonder more recently as an adult?

2. What kinds of activities or events are likely to remind you of your spirit of wonder in your life? (Examples: visiting a far-away place, attending a concert by your favorite musician or musical group, reading to a group of children, flying at 35,000 feet, etc.?)

3. What daily activities make you feel bored, tired, or disinterested? If you can, stop doing them or do less of them.

4. What daily activities do you look forward to doing? Start doing more of them, if you can.

Considerations:

- If you have listed some activities in number 2 above, make plans right now to actually do one of them. Research and find the event, make the reservation, and write it in ink in your planner.
- Think of and find ways that you could help others (especially children) to discover their own spirit and sense of wonder.

7.   APPRECIATE What You Have

∿

This chapter probably sounds very simple to accomplish, but you may find it more of a challenge than you think. Appreciation is exemplified at many different levels and in many different ways.

Consider the day to day conveniences that we all experience – water, electricity, housing, telephones, and television, for starters. A large percentage of the population on our planet does not enjoy the benefits of most of these conveniences.

Appreciation is probably one of the easiest (and most cost-effective) actions you can take on a daily basis. The reason why so few of us do it is probably because it's too easy.

Appreciation requires a conscious effort. It requires you to raise your awareness level for just one moment to say to yourself – "I like the sunshine," or "I like the car I'm driving," or "I love the partner I have," or "I love the profession I'm in," or "I appreciate having the coworkers I have." It's really quite easy, and for this reason you should not put it off.

Because appreciation is initially a conscious effort, you must train yourself to become a habitual appreciator. It may sound silly, but once you get in the habit of consistently appreciating what's around you, life tends to feel just a little

lighter and easier. Appreciating won't take all of your problems away but with your focus now on the positive, more often you tend not to notice the less-than-perfect stuff in your life as much.

You can appreciate anything.

- You can appreciate a thing (a car, house, or a piece of jewelry).
- You can appreciate a person (a parent, sibling, or spouse).
- You can appreciate an experience (a trip, a visit, or a tour).
- You can appreciate the small stuff (a cup of coffee, the sunshine, or the smell of freshly cut grass).

All of these things are there waiting for you to acknowledge them. It is said that the more you appreciate things, the more things God presents to you to appreciate. I believe this. And while it's nice to know that these things are possible, I enjoy the people and things around me because I am grateful for them and because I know there will never be a shortage of things to appreciate.

> *"You may forget from time to time, but you can never unlearn what you experience."*
> — David Dibble

Ways to appreciate what you have:

1. Make a daily ritual out of appreciating things. For example, before starting your car each morning, sit there for a minute and make a list of the things you appreciate at that moment.

2. Who do you most appreciate in your life? Tell them.

3. What do you most appreciate in your life? Why?

Considerations:

- Think back and remember when you felt most grateful for someone or something. Precisely how did it move you and why?
- Once a week, make a serious game out of appreciating things. For one minute, say out loud those things you actively feel appreciation for, no matter how silly they might sound when they first come out of your mouth.
- Learn to appreciate everything – the sun, the weather, the roads you drive, the house you live in, the bed you sleep in, the plates you eat from, the clothes you wear, the family and friends you have, and the air that you breathe. They're all there to appreciate.

8.   Imagine the Possibilities

~

You can chalk it up to conditioning or human nature, but the fact is that we sometimes place more emphasis and attention on what we can't do versus what we can do. While it's important to be realistic and grounded in your daily activities, it is equally important to take the time to have big outlandish thoughts about what could happen in your life — especially if you're intending a specific outcome to occur.

- Where could you go?
- What could you be?
- Who could be your partner?

- What would your life look like after the "mess" is cleaned up?

Okay, I admit I snuck that last one in there to get your attention, but also to get you to start thinking about life after things are corrected, the pain has lessened, and you begin to move past your problem. While you might not believe it right now, it is possible to imagine new possibilities regardless of your current situation. It requires you only to try.

Possibilities emerge when barriers are taken away. In order for you to begin to see what is possible, you first need to imagine your life after your problem is eliminated (or minimized). To do this, you must consciously place your problem to the side. As difficult or impossible-sounding as this might seem, imagine actually taking this problem into your hands and moving its

heavy load into a box. It's a game, yes, but it's a serious game.

Now put this box in a closet. Go ahead and walk to the nearest closet and place your "box of stuff" on the floor of the closet. The intention is not to pretend that you no longer have problems, but to imagine some possibilities without having your problems stacked up next to you.

If your problem is a stack of bills, temporarily put them out of sight. If your problem is too big to move or momentarily avoid, go to a different location – your backyard, the beach, a park, anywhere that allows your mind to become uncluttered and unencumbered.

Once you are ready to imagine, find a comfortable place to sit with no distractions such as TV, music, books, or magazines.

To do this right, you should be able to use the timer on your cell phone or your watch, and set it for 30 minutes. Start the timer and then answer the following question:

> *"If I could go anywhere or do anything with my life, where or what would it be?*

You can have more than one answer to this question. In fact, you may have several. It could be starting a new business or starting a new relationship; it could be changing careers or retiring; it could be getting into the best shape of your life, or it could be writing a book.

Whatever it is, capture it. You have 30 minutes, so stay focused on all the possibilities that surface ... and don't fall into the trap of judging the quality or even the possibility of it ever happening. Some of your responses will be practical and others improbable; it doesn't matter. Go where

your head and your heart are both telling you and write it down.

Mini Centering Prayer – *Lord, allow me to be open enough to actually see and feel the possibilities in my life; especially those I may have suppressed or ignored.*

When the 30-minute alarm sounds, reset the timer for another 30 minutes.

It's time to review your list and sense which ones resonate most with you. Which ones do you find inspiring, challenging, or fun?

Let's say the possibility of changing careers is something that most appeals to you.

If that's the case:

- What would your next career look like?
- What does the job look like?
- Is it a big, small, or medium-sized company?
- Is the position in service, sales, or production?
- What does the culture of the company feel like?
- Is it fast-paced?
- Is it inspiring?
- Is it open-spaced, cubicled, or in an office?
- Is your boss male or female?

If you see the possibility of a new location to live in:

- How do you want to feel when you awake each morning?
- When you're traveling to work each day?

- What are the surroundings you would like to see? (Is it mountains, trees, the ocean, open fields, tall buildings? Maybe snow? Or all of the above?)

Now you see the possibilities. Once you've played with the various aspects of the opportunity you're following, what comes next? A resume, training, researching, networking, or traveling? Regardless of the possibility you are pursuing, it requires thought and planning, and then action and accountability. Your imagination is what moves you forward and out of the proverbial hole you might feel you're in. Much like your values, you must honor the possibility you've imagined by keeping it in front of you and consistently working on it.

Conduct your own personal meeting with yourself each week. Schedule the time and give yourself a solid 45 minutes to review your progress and to consider or reconsider what's next. This is a personal planning session, so treat it seriously.

Some weeks, your progress will be little and other weeks it will feel like you are moving mountains. In either case, keep moving forward, and keep imagining the possibilities at every personal planning session you conduct.

These actions are not intended to resolve your problem, but they will provide more structure and balance in your life while you are dealing with the problem.

Your life is not defined by your problems or your possibilities; your life is defined by how you respond to them. Most often, your

response should be to deal with them creatively, thoughtfully, actively, and aggressively.

In a recent survey conducted informally by a palliative care nurse, the number one regret expressed by dying patients was, "*I wish I'd had the courage to live a life true to myself, not the life others expected of me.*"[1]

Don't let that be you 20, 30, or 40 years from now.

---

1   (In a comment posted to http://www.InspirationandChai.com/ Regrets-of-the-Dying.html by Bonnie Ware, 2011)

Ways to imagine the possibilities:

1.   What times and places are most conducive for you to imagine possibilities for yourself? (Examples – early morning or late at night? By the ocean? By a lake? In a park? In bed? In church? At home, etc.?)

2.   What possibility have you held on to for a long time that has not been realized yet? What is one thing you could do right now that would you move you closer to achieving it?

3.   What do you most wish for as a possibility regarding:
     ○ A future personal or professional relationship?
     ○ A future job?
     ○ A future adventure or travel experience?

Considerations:

- The possibilities we mostly wish for usually include relationships, careers, possessions, situations or experiences, and not always in that order. Work at becoming more mindful about who or what is important to you in your life so that you are more likely to seek out those people and things as future possibilities.
- Take into consideration the possibilities in other people. Too often, we overlook or ignore other people's attempts at imagining possibilities for themselves, or we assume they can't do it. How could you avoid treating someone this way?

9.   Nurture What Is Good in Your Life

~

It's easy and sometimes second nature to focus on the negative things. After all, it seems so easy to spot those things in your life that are less than perfect. I'm not saying to simply "focus on the positive." I am saying recognize what IS good in your life and nurture it! Honor it. Right now.

By doing this, you are not trying to escape your problems; you are looking to quickly move towards that comfortable, consistent place where you know you can be the best person you can be. Even if you feel that everything in your life is in shambles, there will still be good things in your life that you can find. Always! Now is the appropriate time to find and nurture them.

To nurture the good things in your life is to provide care or cultivation; it's a deliberate attempt to help someone or something grow – sometimes selfishly but most times selflessly. Your motivation is not as important as your intention is.

Nurturing is not a regularly occurring activity in most people's lives, mainly because we seldom take the time to consider what really is good in our lives — unless, of course, you have children. If you do, you already know and understand the importance and intention of nurturing.

Do you really know what is good in your life right now? Can you step away from your problem long enough to recognize that God has provided you

with goodness amidst all the less than great stuff, too? It's not easy, but force yourself. Is it your child? Your relationship with your spouse? Your friend? The home or city where you live? Your job? Your boss? Your Coworker? Your neighbor? Your pastor? Your car? Your clothes? Your cooking ability? Your craftsmanship ability? Your hands? Your brains?

- Can you see the importance? The subtlety?
- What is good in your life right now?

A friend of mine owns a Porsche 928. He leads a full and balanced family life and he makes time to enjoy his ride to work each morning. He cares about his car by cleaning and polishing it weekly, and by ensuring it is properly maintained. Does he obsess on his car? Sometimes. Does he love his car more than his family? Never. He knows it's just a car, but he still sees and feels it as something good in his life.

The people in our lives, of course, are a different matter. We can nurture a relationship, but if suddenly that person is not there anymore, it will bother us. It should bother us. People matter. Not to the point of depression or despair but certainly there will be sadness.

Nurturing can simply be doing a little bit extra for that person or thing or performing that activity with a little more care because you have recognized that they are good for you. By this simple act of nurturing, you are lifting yourself above your problems to a higher state of being, one of appreciation and respect.

On another note, we all get out of bed each morning for a reason. Sometimes it's because we feel we have to. But even if your main reason for getting up is going to work, something gets you going on Saturdays and Sundays. What is

it? That's what you want to nurture; that's what needs your focus and attention.

Let's say that you feel you don't have a reason to get out of bed in the morning. What if things seemed horribly wrong in your life at the moment and you don't feel like doing a thing except staying in bed?

What then? Stay in bed! Give yourself one day to indulge, but only one day.

The reality is there will never be a shortage of crappy things that can happen in your life. But that doesn't mean that it's okay to dwell on them for very long. Consciously choose to focus on the good stuff, don't ignore or avoid the bad, but keep yourself on the *glass-half-full* side of life.

IMPORTANT NOTE: *We all experience a time where we feel down or despondent. But if your lack of desire to do anything lasts for more than a couple of weeks, you need to seek professional help. Someone who can accurately and competently diagnose and help remedy your problem. When your resilience to bounce back does not arrive in a timely manner, your ability to help yourself is diminished and an outside professional viewpoint is your best next step.*

Ways to nurture what is good in your life:

1. Despite your current situation, what is good in your life right now? It could be as simple as having food on the table, no matter how little. What are those things? List them.
2. Who is a positive force in your life? How do you or how can you nurture and reinforce this relationship?
3. What kinds of things are you really good at? What are you complimented on regularly? How could you nurture this skill or ability?

Considerations:

- Call three people you haven't spoken to in the last six months just to see how they are. (Again, resist the temptation to tell them your problem, though. You want their company, not their pity.) Catch up on old times; share new stuff; reconnect. By the third call you'll be wondering why you hadn't called these people months ago.
- What activities or sports do you find beneficial and/or enjoyable? Actively look for ways to be able to do them more often.

10. Evolve, Don't Change

∿

When confronted with a serious problem or challenge, our first inclination is to do what is necessary to fix it immediately. If, at first glance it appears that you must change in order to correct things, recognize that this may not be the response that's needed.

Many people resist evolving because they are impatient; they simply will not wait for the desired remedy or result. It has to be now; so they change either themselves or the situation. But change usually requires force, and evolving is not forced. When a person evolves, there is a slower, more meaningful, more lasting transformation that takes place.

There are, however, those situations that absolutely require immediate change, and they have little to do with transformation. Things like taking medication to treat a serious illness, or taking your car in for service because the "check engine" light came on; deciding not to use your credit card if you're having financial difficulties; or seeing a doctor (or other appropriate professional) if you're feeling physically, emotionally, or spiritually unwell. These are all examples of situations that you cannot and should not wait to evolve; you must change.

The evolving actions that you take actually come in the form of being proactive. This means taking slow, deliberate steps towards making something happen over the course of time – months, even

years – where the effects can have a meaningful impact on your life.

Some examples of evolving actions include: exercising and eating right, having scheduled maintenance done on your automobile, contributing to a regular savings plan, and having regular medical checkups.

Other ways we evolve have to do with our habits and behaviors. These include the exercise we perform, the foods we eat or don't eat, the rest we get, the spirituality we practice, the relationships we foster and contribute to, and the livelihood we seek or choose.

Sometimes, we seek to evolve in how we respond to people and events. If you have a particular behavior you don't like in yourself, you cannot simply choose to stop behaving that way; you must go through a process of raising your awareness about which situations cause this behavior and then consciously take steps to respond differently versus just reacting (or overreacting).

As a way to bring more light into your life, consider the distinction between patience and just tolerating someone's behavior. In no way does this mean if you experience someone's rude or unkind behavior that you simply ignore or avoid it. Your evolved response should take into consideration a balanced action versus an outburst of activity. In other words, don't meet unkind behavior with unkind behavior. Defend your boundaries, let people know when they have crossed the line with you, and then let it go. Move on. Get busy with whatever it was that held your attention before the other person appeared.

Evolving is a strategy you can employ in many areas of your life, and it can work especially well when you're dealing with a big problem. When a big challenge is staring you in the face, rather than fighting it or fleeing from it, take a quick account of things. Rise above it, if you can, and try to look at it with an outsider's set of eyes.

Ask yourself – "How can I deal with this problem in a measured and balanced way?" a way that will allow for adjustments as time passes, but still leaves you feeling that you are effectively dealing with it and making progress at the same time. Evolving can sometimes mean making subtle adjustments in your life versus making extreme or radical changes.

Ways to evolve:

1. Practice patience. We all have been conditioned to get things as soon as we want them. That rarely happens. Pick something you have wanted to change about yourself, and slowly begin to change.

2. Watch for signs. People and things evolve around us all the time; we usually miss the signals because we don't take the time to really look at people and things or fully listen to people.

3. Identify what makes you feel happy, and content; conversely, notice what causes the opposite feelings to occur. Were you already aware of these triggers?

Considerations:

- Learning to pay closer attention to those around you and how you respond to them is a big step towards evolving more quickly and completely. Look carefully to see if their words match their actions, or vice versa.
- Another way to evolve is being aware when someone is annoying you. Try to catch yourself in the act of feeling annoyed before you respond. Making a game out of catching yourself in the act will raise your awareness level to new heights and may even get people to notice there is something different about you.

Centering Prayer #4

~

Dear God, help me to be more patient.

Help me find the kind of patience that allows me not just to change but to grow and evolve into the person I wish to be. I know in some ways I'm already there, but I also know that patience will help me stay there.

Help me to understand and appreciate how other people evolve as well. I want to recognize and acknowledge the positive change and growth of people around me. Help me to be more aware of their conscious efforts so that I may learn from them.

My intention is to improve how I respond to my inner thoughts, as well as to the actions and words of other people who could trigger a negative response in me.

Help me to learn both patience and understanding versus only tolerance and suppressing myself.

11. Solutions!

~

Like most of us, you probably want a fast solution to your problem. Sometimes, when we're looking for a quick fix in order to stop the pain, discomfort, or embarrassment, we miss the obvious. What initially appeared to be a good solution comes back to bring us more problems.

Don't misunderstand; sometimes the quick fix really is the right solution. It's a trick of the eye, so to speak. Because we are so compelled to rid ourselves of this problem, we will convince ourselves very quickly that this is the solution. Solutions take time. Not weeks or months, but at least a few days of contemplation, soul searching, prayer, reflection, and research. Only then should you proceed.

Note: If your situation has an imminent deadline, then obviously you're going to need to reduce the time necessary to research and reflect.

To help you avoid paralysis by analysis, the following questions are provided to guide you through the basics of identifying and implementing a solution.

- On the surface, does the solution you have identified make sense? (Or is it just a case of wishful thinking?)
- Do you feel the solution has at least an 80% chance of working? (Or is it a case of wishful thinking?)

- Will the solution cause any additional problems?
- (If yes, are you prepared to deal with them right away?)
- Will the solution adversely affect other people?
- (If yes, talk to those affected for their input.)
- Have you considered all aspects of the situation? Are you certain there are no other options?
- Is there a way to ensure that this problem will never come back?
- Have you sought the counsel of those who may be able to guide you? (Or are you operating in a vacuum of shame, embarrassment, or ego?)
- Have you mapped out the steps you need to take, along with an estimated timetable for completion?

- If this is the right solution, and it works:
  - ○ How will your life be different?
  - ○ What will change for you in the short term?
  - ○ What will change for you in the long term?

12. The First Day of the Rest of Your Life

~

Much of what you have read in the preceding pages was about your response to events and feelings in your life. Those responses will never stop. From this day forward, you should become more responsible for how you consciously and unconsciously respond to things. You know better. There should be no more hiding from your problems without realizing that you are only hurting yourself by doing so.

One of the Four Noble Truths in Buddhism is that we all suffer. While this may sound harsh, the intention behind the truth is to acknowledge that suffering is there, and then move on; but never forget that it's still there. Another way of saying this is – "Don't let suffering control your life, but don't take it for granted, either."

Again, it's all about how you respond to events in your life. You can be determined to constantly seek inspiration in your life, or you can decide to allow yourself to feel miserable and unhappy.

You can decide to be a creator of better circumstances, or you can be a victim of circumstance.

You can actively seek out as many good things as you can in life, or you can spend your time to focusing on the things you consider bad.

You can directly face what you fear, see it for what it is, and get on with living your life, or you can allow fear to take hold and immobilize you.

Your life is not defined by your problems; your life is defined by you. You can always let your problems define your life, but the preference should *always* be to consciously choose to redefine your life.

In each case, your response is your choice. Choose wisely. Act consistently on your choices and seek outside support and feedback on a regular basis to ensure you're not fooling yourself with your choices.

13. The Triple Threat – <u>Frustration</u>, <u>Confusion</u>, and <u>Feeling Overwhelmed</u>

～

Perhaps you are in a "perfect storm" situation right now – you are facing the triple threat – too many problems, you don't know where you are, your compass is broken, and you've lost your map. It happens to people more frequently than you may think.

This is not the time to break down and give up. Instead, it's time to shake off whatever is clinging to you at the moment and give yourself some time and space to evaluate your situation.

Upon review, your situation might be bad; in fact, it might be miserable. But God has given you a mind and a body to think and act. That means you have the know-how and the ability to get out of the way if something is about to hit you, or to slam on the brakes if you're about to crash into something.

I'm being overly simplistic to make a point. Almost every problem can be broken down to its simplest form and addressed. It takes time, it takes energy, and it takes courage to do this, but…it must be done.

Now, let's consider the triple threat. Most big problems will affect you in one, two, or three of the following ways – frustration, confusion, and/or feeling overwhelmed. The first two, frustration and confusion, can affect you almost immediately when a problem occurs, but feeling overwhelmed

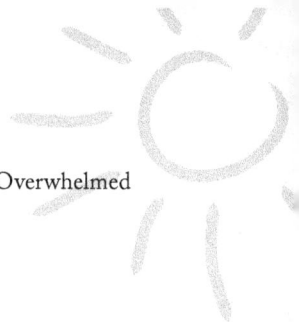

takes time. Like wine fermenting in a barrel, the seeds of becoming overwhelmed get planted in plain sight, right in front of you, but you're usually too preoccupied with other things to recognize it for what it is.

Frustration – If you're at the point with your problem right now where you're feeling frustrated, that's good. Frustration is really a warning sign for things to come. It's telling you that if you don't do something, eventually what is frustrating you may get worse. It's the same as that strange sound coming from the back end of your car when you drive, or the kitchen faucet starting to leak. They both may be frustrating to experience, but if left unchecked, they could result in even bigger problems.

Frustration, too, can come from things that are more pressing – the possibility of losing your job, an antagonistic boss or coworker, or a bill that is incorrect and you can't find the right person to correct it for you. Each one of these frustrating situations, if they continue, will wear you down, and possibly could become an even bigger problem.

Confusion – Sometimes it doesn't take much to get confused. With the complexities of the world bearing down on you more than ever before, it is easy to miss the obvious – a sign, an instruction, a recommendation or direction. You may be preoccupied with a task that you are working on and then suddenly discover it's an hour later than you thought and you miss an important meeting.

Or maybe you have experienced a time when you had too many obligations and a problem or two thrown in on top of things, and then you are not sure what to do next. It happens to a

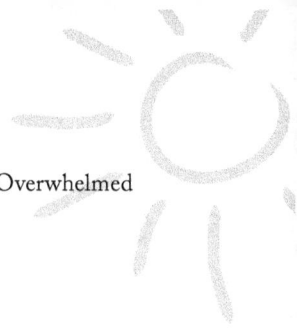

lot of people. Your first reaction may need to be one that is re-learned. You may need to take a moment to disengage from whatever you are doing and reflect. Say to yourself, "What's going on here?" And then give yourself a few minutes to listen for an answer.

Feeling Overwhelmed – Feeling overwhelmed comes when you are frustrated (with yourself, with things, with people, with everything) and you are also confused. Not the minor confusion that can happen daily, but heavy duty confusion of the first order. It is at times like these when you may be at your emotional, physical, and spiritual low points, and the triple threat hits you square in the stomach.

When you become overwhelmed, it hits hard, and you will go down. The question is for how long?

Recognize that the above examples, in general, are not big problems or issues. Most, in fact, are resolvable through a routine phone call or conversation. A leaky faucet, for example, is not cause to stop what you're doing and call the plumber immediately. When you realize that something is frustrating you, stop and consider what really is happening and keep things in perspective. Overreacting to something that's frustrating will actually cause more problems in your life.

In some situations, like dealing with an antagonistic coworker, you will have to decide if it's really worth the effort to deal with the issue because even your best conversation may not change that person's mind or attitude. You may just have to deal with it, be frustrated, and eventually look for another position.

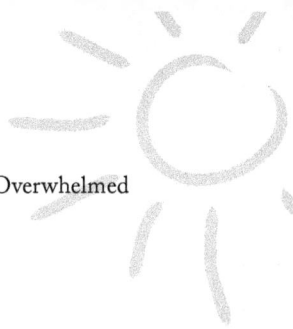

When you believe all three elements of the triple threat are in existence in your life, don't give up. Tackle each one, one by one, and follow the previously outlined steps.

You are bigger than you problems.

14. The Last Word

~

After you've indulged and you've stopped feeling sorry for yourself, after you've commiserated with friends or relatives, after you've cried yourself out, you may feel utterly exhausted by the ordeal. But you must wake up one day and say to yourself – "I'm going to deal with my stuff!"

Remember Chapter 2, **"Your Situation IS YOURS,"** which was about accepting responsibility for your "stuff," or your problems? Well, this is it. This is THE MOMENT for you to step up, shake off whatever feelings are dragging you down, and renew your commitment to resolving your stuff.

Make your lists, consider your intended actions, take action, be aware, look for signs of what's working and what's not, and be happy.

And don't forget to thank God for what you do have.

Acknowledgments

Many people have helped me with the creation of this book.

I would especially like to thank the following individuals: Monte Lambert, Irene Revelas, Stephen Garber, Steve Shannon, Matt Peace, Greg Behl, Jeff Hooker, Doug Peace, Tom Tardonia and Herb Ammons.

A special thank you to my daughter, Vanessa, for her cover design; and to my wife, Maura, who has helped me throughout the writing process and beyond.

Life can be turbulent at times, but with good friends, a loving family, and an intentional attitude of gratitude, sunshine will prevail.

May we all be the light that we wish to see in the world.

About the Author

Jeff Pasquale is an Executive and Life Coach who works specifically in the areas of life, leadership, and legacy. He has been coaching for 20 years.

He lives in Boynton Beach, Florida.

More information about Jeff can be found at www.JeffPasquale.com

He is the author of: *The Book of Leader: A Testament to the Art of Leadership*, *The Magic Dance: Do You Lead, Follow, or Get Out of the Way?*, *How BIG is Your Target?: The Power of Focus in a Cluttered World*, *Looking for*

SUNSHINE: *A Practical Guide for Dealing with Life's Challenges,* ***Subway Life:*** *An Underground Guide to Balanced Living,* ***Get That Promotion:*** *Manage Up and Get There Faster,* and ***Get That New Job:*** *Self-Coaching Steps That Work.*

www.ingramcontent.com/pod-product-compliance
Lightning Source LLC
Chambersburg PA
CBHW060301050426
42448CB00009B/1719